SOLD OUT FOR SUCCESS

Keys to Living a
Dynamic Life in Christ

Everett Marshall

© Copyright by Everett Marshall - 2019

All rights reserved

No part of this publication may be reproduced or transmitted in any form or by any means; electronic or mechanical, including photocopying, and recording without the written permission from the Author and/or the publishers.

TABLE OF CONTENTS

PART I

CHAPTER 1   What is the meaning of success? 7

CHAPTER 2   Are you willing to do what it takes? 13

CHAPTER 3   What's your level of dedication? 19

CHAPTER 4   Worthwhile goals 31

CHAPTER 5   Success Leaves Clues 33

CHAPTER 6   You Were Born to Succeed 41

CHAPTER 7   Success feels good. 45

CHAPTER 8   Total Life Success 53

PART II

CHAPTER 9   Eternal Success 57

CHAPTER 10   Keys to living a Dynamic Life for Christ . . 59

CHAPTER 11   Jesus the Prayer Champion 61

CHAPTER 12   Daniel the Leader on Fasting 67

CHAPTER 13 Are you devoted to the word
            like the first church? 73

CHAPTER 14 Giving like Solomon 77

CHAPTER 15 Mercy, Mercy Me. 81

CHAPTER 16 Success-Imagine That!! 83

CHAPTER 17 Success – Will you sacrifice
            your Isaac to go higher?. 85

CHAPTER 18 Fighters mentality 91

CHAPTER 19 Endurance with Job 93

CHAPTER 20 Stay Connected to the Vine. 97

CHAPTER 21 Two Roads Diverge. 101

Conclusion 105

PART I

PART

CHAPTER 1

What is the meaning of success?

Have you ever wondered what it would take for you to hit the bullseye on your way to mammoth success in life? Have you tried to find success in life, only to get pushed back, again and again?

Success is defined as the accomplishment of an aim or purpose. My definition of success is the attainment of certain statutes, goals, and line-markers in life. It could be finishing writing or reading a particular book. It could be getting out of debt or becoming a better person. Success is different for everyone. So how should the believer in Christ view their personal success? Or through what lens do they need to view success from? The Bible says,

> *"But seek ye first His kingdom and His righteousness, and all these things will be added to you."-Matthew 6:33*

For me, success has been walking in my calling in God and reaching a certain level of financial prosperity to be able to bless the Kingdom of God and leave an inheritance for my children's children. To some that might seem vain and meaningless. But in my 40 years I have realized that a lot of problems in the world can be solved with money. A lack of money has ruined the fortunes of countless people. I always knew that when I became rich and wealthy, I would be dedicated to helping others in the world reach financial success. You see, many believe that the financially successful are stingy and tight fisted. But that can't be further from the truth. The wealthy in this nation are some of the greatest philanthropist known in the world. They have foundations and charities that give to countless causes in the world. But attaining wealth and philanthropy should not be the sole purpose and reason that the believer measures their success in life. True success is obeying and following the will of God on your life as He grows us, matures us, and takes us from glory to glory.

Many are seeking the things before seeking His righteousness. Worrying about the mundane things in life has called us to take our focus off the will of God and focus solely on getting our immediate needs met. He has promised that if we make His kingdom and righteousness our top priority then He would make sure to add everything we need to live a successful life. If you don't believe me, let's look at what His word says.

Psalms 112:1-3

> "Praise the Lord!
> Blessed is the man who fears the Lord,
> Who delights greatly in His commandments?
> His descendants will be mighty on earth;
> The generation of the upright will be blessed.
> Wealth and riches will be in his house,
> And his righteousness endures forever.
> Wealth and riches shall be in His house."

This psalm deals with one of the biggest challenges facing the children of God today. Look at the second line – "Blessed is the man who fears the Lord." When you're reading the Word, and it says "Blessed be …" you know you're going to want to keep reading.

When God says, "Blessed be," he is talking to a large problem facing his church or children, and that problem is usually the characteristic that is opposite whomever he is declaring blessed. This case of this psalm, God is speaking to a person with a very specific problem. A problem that seems to get attention in the book of Psalms on a regular basis.

Here, God is talking about people that fear anything more than the Lord.

It could be anything.

Your boss. Your wife. The weather. The recession. Anything. But, in this scripture, he's not telling you the things you're going to receive as a result of fearing something more than the Lord. Here, he's giving you a carrot. He's telling you what you'll get if you change your ways. And what you're going to be getting sounds pretty good to me.

Here's what he is saying:

"If you fear Me, and you do more than just obey My commandments. You must want to keep my commandments. You must find joy in doing what I say you should do. If you do this, I'm going to bless you. I'm going to bless your descendants. And I'm going to do even more. I'm going to bless everyone on the earth that is good, that does what he's supposed to be doing.?

Then, he tells us what his blessings are going to be. He promises wealth and riches in the home of the person that loves to follow Him. The righteousness you show, is going to get passed down to your kids and their kids. And the Lord's house will get blessed as wall.

In other words, if we faithfully follow God and seek His greater good first, prosperity and abundance shall be our portion.

Just remember, and this is probably the most difficult part of this Psalm: you HAVE TO delight greatly in the Lord's commandments.

The word of God also says this, and it's from 1 Timothy 6:17:

"Command those who are rich in this present age not to be haughty, nor to trust in uncertain riches but in the living God, who gives us richly all things to enjoy."

This scripture sounds awfully like the psalm we just went over, but the intended audience is a little bit different. If you look, the instruction is directed towards those who have already found wealth. But you'll also notice that it talks about trust.

Trust is something that is extended towards someone or something that consistently gives us a result that we desire. If we trust something, we expect that something is going to follow through when we need it.

The word here tells us that wealth, prestige, and all that other stuff that comes with it, is uncertain. It can be here in a moment, and it can leave us even quicker. It tells us to trust the Lord.

There are some things that God wants to give us to enjoy. The scripture says God wants to give us richly all things to enjoy. This is the abundant life that Jesus wants us to walk in. He wants us to have more than enough money, good health, good relationships, thriving marriages, a healthy family, a sound mind, and much more.

This is the type of success we need to walk in. And we can, but we need to trust God first.

My attempt in this book is not to help you locate what your definition of success is. Your definition of success is something you'll have to figure out yourself. It's not something I can define for you. Your life is too unique, to special, for me to do that.

Instead, I want to give you the Biblical keys to attain the success you desire.

You see, your definition of success should be so powerful that it causes you to wake up in the middle of the night and work at it. If it's not that strong, you need to reassess it, and figure out what would keep you up in the middle of the night.

You need to find something that will give you the drive to stick with it through the hard times that are going to come.

Additionally, you'll need a burning passion for something else. You need to have a passion for the Kingdom and His righteousness. If you don't, chances are high that sticking with your vision for success will be difficult to maintain, especially when the roads get rough.

CHAPTER 2

Are you willing to do what it takes?

Have you ever wanted something really bad? Something you wanted so bad you were willing to do anything you could in order to make it work. I'm willing to bet that you got it done. I'm also willing to bet not all of your endeavors ended with the same kind of result.

There's nothing wrong with that.

But you need to know that there is a reason for that, and that reason is exactly what this chapter is all about.

The first principle that we need to look at in the attainment of success is willingness. If you are willing to do whatever it takes, you will find the ability to do so.

There is a difference in desiring to do whatever it takes and having a willingness to do so. For example, I can want to go outside and cut the grass. But my willingness to cut the grass can be quenched as I focus on how hot it is outside, how long it will take, and I could simply pay someone to do it. The Kingdom of God does not work like this.

Nevertheless, your willingness to take on an endeavor can be found if you weigh the risks versus rewards of not doing it. Case in point, I can either diligently pursue my business or not. The consequences can be a successful system, unlimited profits, freedom from the shackles of a 9 to 5, and an inheritance to pass down. If I choose not to do it, the shackles of a job remain, I will be subjected to someone else's rules and regulations, and no inheritance to pass down. Isaiah 1:19

If you are willing and obedient, you shall eat the good of the land;

Trying times and rough roads are going to face anyone who attempts any worthwhile endeavor. I know this from experience.

Growing up, I was the chubby kid in school and received ridicule for it. By the time I had reached my teenage years I had had enough of the ridicule, jokes, and negative attention that comes with being overweight. I was inspired to do something about it. At that stage of my life, I determined that success for me was losing a whole lot of weight in order to look a certain way. If I looked a certain way, I believed that the ridicule would stop, and I would be appealing to the opposite sex. But regardless of that, I still had to do something about it.

I remember as if it was yesterday even though it was over 20 years ago. I would struggle to get up in the morning and go to the gym. I would struggle to stay on some type of healthy eating plan. It was a constant struggle to not weigh myself every day. There was a huge emotional struggle when the scale went 5 pounds in any direction. And you know what? Something had to give.

I could not keep up the struggle. I had to make a choice, or that choice was going to be made fore me. And I'll tell you what, it wasn't going to be the result that got me skinny again.

But that choice was not an easy one. I was getting slammed by doubts.

Doubts about whether the diet and exercise were worth it – especially with my slow and mostly mediocre results. Doubts about whether I was worth the effort it was taking to get myself in shape. Doubts about whether anyone even cared about what I was doing.

There were times I just wanted to give up right there and go back to what I was doing before.

But then I remembered something. I remembered what I wanted. I remembered my goal. I remembered how I felt every time I looked into a mirror, and how embarrassed I was at school when I would walk down the halls.

Something clicked.

That success that I wanted – the success where I was healthy, skinny, and all that turned itself up a notch. It became more than just a want, more than just a desire. It turned into a burning desire. And I got driven.

I found that, regardless of the struggle, I was determined to lose the weight and keep it off. Believe it or not, it's 20 years later and it's easy for me to get up in the morning or evening and workout for an hour. But that took years of grit and determination.

Many make New Year's resolutions but fail to act on them. If they do act on them, they give up at the smallest hint of failure or danger. But like the old saying goes, "If you fall off the wagon, simply get back on". I believe that we don't get back up because of two reasons.

First, we don't get back up because we failed to properly plan and count the cost of what it takes. I've seen it over and over again. People get excited about something. The get so excited they can't contain the enthusiasm, and they jump right in. But, after a couple of months, something else happens.

They realize getting what they wanted is going to take longer than they thought. They get an idea about how long it may take to actually get what they want, and they get discouraged. The drive to accomplish it diminishes to something much smaller. They find that the price to get what they want is actually more than they were willing to pay.

This could have been avoided by doing two simple things.

All you need to do, once you figure out what you want to accomplish, is make a plan, and figure out what it will cost to get it done. Then you can start "doing."

Second, our desire to attain that success is not strong enough. This one is a little different problem, but it's equally difficult to overcome. When you want something bad enough, you'll get it done. But doing things that give us this much "desire" doesn't come around very often.

Instead, we do things that we know would be good for us, or that would help us out, but that we don't really want to do. Me losing weight all those years ago is a good example of this. I wanted to lose weight, but the cost of losing that weight nearly overpowered my desire to get it done.

Like it was with me, when the allure of not getting things done, and keeping everything status quo is bigger than your desire to get what you want. You are not going to get it done. Unfortunately, most people don't figure out that they'd rather not do anything months or years into their endeavor.

And when that happens, it's really hard to get back on track.

But there is hope. Read this quote from someone who knows what it's like to succeed and fail.

"I suppose the secret to bouncing back is not only to be unafraid of failures but to use them as motivational and learning tools. ... There's nothing wrong with making mistakes as long as you don't make the same ones over and over again."- Richard Branson

You see, it's not in your successes that you actually "succeed." It's actually in how you deal with your failures. Failure and struggle should motivate you to get back on the plate and swing again after a miss. Are you give up after you have two strikes against you. Are you going to throw in the towel after you strike out once?

Twice?

Three times?

If you have a history of throwing in the towel, or you feel like you might be close, it's time you took a look at your level of dedication to achieving your goal.

CHAPTER 3

What's your level of dedication?

Have you ever seen the movie "Rocky?"

It's a good one.

In that movie, a washed-up boxer, one without much motivation or drive, somehow gets the chance to fight the world heavyweight champion. He was out of shape, overweight, and didn't have a chance to succeed. But he was able to put up an amazing fight.

The only thing was, he never would have been able to succeed without a rededication of his life to the things that mattered most. He had to get back to the basics. He had to make things right between him and his trainer, and him and Adrian. For you, it's no different. But, since this isn't Hollywood, your basics need to come from somewhere else.

They need to come from the Lord.

Once you have cultivated a strong spiritual life and consecration, then you can begin to focus on your personal success. It cannot be the other way around. I have found that as you serve the Lord and seek His way, He begins to reveal what your deepest values and desires are. So how does it look when we take our focus off the Lord and focus strictly on the mundane in life?

"Then the devil, taking Him up on a high mountain, showed Him all the kingdoms of the world in a moment of time. And the devil said to Him, "All this authority I will give You, and their glory; for this has been delivered to me, and I give it to whomever I wish. Therefore, if you will worship before me, all will be yours." And Jesus answered and said to him, "Get behind Me, Satan! For it is written, you shall worship the Lord your God, and Him only you shall serve."—Luke 4:5-8

One of our enemies' primary goals is to get you to follow self-will versus God's will. When we do this, we forsake divine destiny. In the short term, we can find a certain level of success by chasing our own will. But this type of success is not durable or fulfilling. God wants to give you durable hope, good success, and blessings that will overtake you. You just need to know how to find these things.

Now in practicality, your level of dedication to success shows off in your everyday habits and actions. You can't tell me you are serious about going back to school if you don't register or fill out an application. You can't tell me you are serious about making money if you are not seeking employment or exercising diligence in your business affairs. You can't tell me you are serious about your health if you fail to use moderation in your eating habits and drink and smoke daily. Your success encapsulates your total being. I have come to believe that you should want to be successful in every area of your life, including marriage, parenting, money, health, and spiritual well-being.

This comes from personal experience.

I have not always been totally dedicated to success in my health.

There was a time when I was overweight, drank too much, and partied all night until the sun came up. It was easy to do, because I was having a good time. A really good time. But things didn't stay rosy for me. The repercussions of my actions started showing up.

And they usually showed up at the most inopportune times.

As is frustratingly normal in these kinds of situations, my habits and hobbies started to compete with things that I needed to get done. I was having to choose between staying out late and partying and spending time with people I cared about. And choosing between these things was really, really difficult.

It got to the point where I found myself choosing the pleasurable option more often that I wanted to admit, and my life was suffering. Things I wanted to achieve started playing second fiddle, and I was finally put in a spot where I had to choose one thing over the other. The time of serving two masters was about to come to an end.

But who was I going to choose?

Fortunately, since you're reading this story, it's clear that I was able to pull myself up and choose the right thing. But it was one of the toughest choices of my life. But now, there's no turning back.

Once I realized that my spiritual health and bodily health were important, I made significant changes to my daily habits. For example, I cut down on my intake of white carbs, soda, candy, and fast food. I then began to drink more water and less soft drinks and juice. I worked out more and gradually the weight began to come off. These minor shifts in my habits caused great shifts in my health and well-being.

Tony Robbins said, "The path to success is to take massive, determined action".

When we look at the life of Jesus, we can observe that He was busy doing the Father's work. Jesus "went about doing good". If the determination to see something accomplished is there, you can will yourself to making changes, overcoming obstacles, and sticking to your plan for success. So, what does a plan for success look like? Your plan can have as little as 4-5 habits that you choose to implement in your daily life. A habit is defined as a settled or regular tendency or practice, especially one that is hard to give up. The interesting fact about habits is that they can be good or bad. You can take up the habit of eating fruit daily or smoking a pack of cigarettes daily.

Let's discuss habits a little more in detail. In an informative article from Forbes magazine, they claim that habits are all structured one from another. They go on to say that all habits can be broken down into three basic components.

The first of these components is the Cue or Trigger.

The cue or trigger is the part of the habit loop where you are triggered to take some sort of action through a cue in your internal or external environment. Without these triggers, these habit loops would never start. Unfortunately, ANYTHING can be a trigger.

For example, let's say you have a bad habit of not cutting your lawn in a timely manner. And just for fun let's say your neighborhood Homeowners Association sends you letters in the mail periodically to warn you that there are penalties for failing to keep your lawn maintained and manicured. Oh, and I forgot to mention that your neighbors tend to give you dirty looks when your grass gets a little too high. One of your neighbors, the guy that's won the "Lawn of the Year" award for the last 12 years give you the words look of them all. These could very well be the trigger or triggers that lead you to cutting your lawn on a consistent basis.

The second component in the habit is loop the Action. Good or bad, this is the part of the habit loop where you actually take action on the habit you want to adopt or drop. It's the thing you do because of that nasty trigger. Looking back at our example of the poorly manicured lawn, because of the snarls, snickers, and dirty HOA letters you have received, you internally decide to take action and maintain your lawn.

The final component is the Reward. This is the part of the habit loop where your brain receives a reward for taking the desired activity. If you think about it another way, your reward could act as both your trigger and your reward. To continue the lawn example, you manicure your law every day, and do such a good job, you incidentally win that "Lawn of the Year" award, and knock that annoying neighbor off his pedestal, finally get some praise from your neighbors, or even the pride you feel from taking better care of your property.

Charles Duhigg, the author of "The Power of Habit", and an expert on behavioral psychology, suggests that most people fail to adopt new habits because they do not understand the structure of habits. More specifically, most people fail to adequately reward themselves for taking action on a beneficial habit."

So, what he is saying is that you should reward yourself after you develop a new habit and begin seeing results. Say for example you begin a diet and exercise program and begin to start losing weight and seeing more tone and definition. You could continually eat like a rabbit everyday but that could lead to burnout and frustration. Instead, to reward yourself why not have a "cheat day or cheat meal". You could take one meal out of one day of the week to indulge in whatever your favorite food is. This cheat meal will motivate you, encourage you, and strengthen you to continue sticking to your new habit, even some of the more difficult habits out there.

If you look at the reality of most addictive and destructive habits, you can see they have a built-in reward system that requires little or no input from you. For example, smoking a cigarette, snorting cocaine, or drinking yourself into oblivion are all easy habits to adopt because they light up your brain with a slew of pleasure chemicals.

The chemicals that get released from using these substances are normally released during specific activities you can do. Activities like exercise, sleeping, completing a huge task, or even sex. These substances allow these chemicals to get released from your brain without you needing to anything other than ingesting them. As a result, these substances naturally reward your brain and encourage continued usage even though they are detrimental to your overall health and well-being.

On the other hand, many positive habits such as exercise, meditation, focused work, and healthy eating don't have immediately obvious rewards. Unless you know why you do these things, your reward is going to come later. To the person that lives day-to-day, pursuing one pleasure to the next, the reasons for undertaking these kinds of good activities will be a mystery.

So herein lies the difference between a good habit and a bad habit. Bad habits tend to give us instant reward and gratification. Good habits establish patterns that will allow us to obtain greater things in life – things that don't require you to undertake destructive behaviors that can harm you and others. The difference between these two kinds of habits will also help you discern between good and bad activities.

As a general rule, those things that require work, persistence, and patience, are habits that you are going to want to spend time developing. However, developing these habits is much more difficult than developing the bad ones.

That is the reason why so many of us have developed these bad of habits. For example, smoking, overeating, laziness, too much television, and so on. On the other hand, good habits like healthy eating, exercise, goal setting, and positive thinking require patience and diligence in order to see results.

Did you know that on average, it takes about a week to lose one to two pounds of body fat? And this is with a strong dedication to diet and a workout routine. On the flip side, while I write this book, I can order a meat lovers pizza with extra cheese, have it delivered, eat the whole pie, and watch my favorite movie or television show online all at the same time.

What a world we live in.

That which we need less of is easily accessible to us. But that which takes effort can sometimes be elusive and hard to achieve.

My point in giving this information is for you to take an active awareness of what triggers your fancy. What internal or external cues nudge you into a sedentary and goal forsaking existence? If you are struggling to make a new habit stick, then you probably aren't aware or consciously applying the habit loop to change it.

Remember, ALL habits have some kind of trigger. Most of the time, most people don't even realize these triggers are there – silently helping them do things that may not be in their best interest. Here are a few examples:

For one person, driving down a specific street will make him want to buy donuts, because as a kid he only ever went down that street to buy donuts. For another person, the glares from his neighbors could be enough to make him mow his law. For another person, the ads at the bottom of a specific website could trigger him to want to take a look at some inappropriate websites later that day.

When we're talking about these triggers, they can be identified.

It just takes a little bit of work.

In order to figure out what your triggers are, you need to figure out what habits you're trying to break. So, first, figure out those habits you want to change. The next thing you need to do is relive the last time you did that habit.

Go from start to finish.

Then, once that's over, take a break. This could be a difficult exercise – and you're not done yet. The next thing you need to do is go back to the very beginning of that experience. You need to think about what you were doing before you started the habit.

It could have been anything.

Then you need to thing about what you were thinking about. If you have to think about it for a while, that's fine. Once you figure it out, then you need to write it down. Chances are, the thing you were doing right before that habit started is your trigger. If you're still not sure, think about another time you did that habit. Go to the beginning and try to remember what you were doing then.

If you do this enough, you'll start to see a pattern. Once you see that pattern, you'll be able to use that knowledge to avoid that rigger altogether.

"Sticking to good habits can be hard work, and mistakes are part of the process. Don't declare failure simply because you messed up or because you're having trouble reaching your goals. Instead, use your mistakes as opportunities to grow stronger and become better."-Amy Morin

This seems easy, but we make it harder than it has to be. It just takes will and determination. The masses refuse to be disciplined in life because the payoff is too great to continue doing what they are doing. The masses get complacent and comfortable in life and that's why change never comes.

Changing or adding one positive habit to your daily life can have lasting effects for you for years to come. For example, in regard to your health, if you decided to cut back on sweets and your sugar intake you could easily lose up to 10 pounds or more and greatly reduce your risk of diabetes and other diseases as you get older. If instead of spending every dollar you make, you can add the habit of saving $100 a month. After a year you could have over $1000 saved. If you invest that $1000 correctly you could have extra income to do whatever you'd like with.

Sometimes we believe we have to make drastic changes in order to see results, but this isn't always the case. I know without a doubt that this works. Now what I'm about to say might sound arrogant but there is a lot of truth to it and it goes to show you what happens over time. When I first began to eat right and exercise regularly it was a long and arduous journey. Some days or mornings I literally had to force myself to go to the gym and moderate what I ate and what I didn't eat. I look back on those early days and chuckle because now these same tasks are easy for me. It takes almost no will power for me to get up early and go to the gym for an hour. It takes no will power for me to watch my portions and eat right. If I can do it, anyone can. Success isn't for someone from a certain background, family, or neighborhood. Success waits for anyone who is willing to reach out and grab it.

Anyone can reach for the "low hanging fruits" in life. You might ask what are low hanging fruits? Low hanging fruits are that which is easy to grab because it is low hanging or easily accessible. I would relate this to applying for a low paying job or settling for average when you can have better and best. Fruits that hang high cost you something. These types of fruits cause you to stretch, climb, and seek greater strategies to obtain. These types of fruits make you feel elated and have a since of pride once you obtain or accomplish them. Examples of high hanging fruits are a high paying job, starting and running a business, going to the college you desire, obtaining the exact type of spouse you want, etc.

Do you know what settling for low hanging fruits does? It makes you apathetic and desensitized about how much wonder life has to offer. Many don't know and understand that there is greater out there for them. Their greater is just around the corner from reaching. Even in my own life I have had to reach and grab that which I desired. For example, for a 4-year period I went from lackluster job to lackluster job. Even though every new opportunity gave me a slight pay raise I knew there was greater out there for me. So instead of settling for mediocrity I began to search out an even better opportunity. I began to step out and take evaluations with better companies and low and behold they allowed me to continue in their hiring process. But my job wasn't finished there. I literally had to apply for over 20 positions until one fell through. Day after day I would apply like a mad man. My wife thought I was crazy. But eventually after a 2-year waiting period I got my chance. I was offered the best job I have had this far. And to be honest, it was all worth it.

But many think that success is going to happen to them overnight. When I give people my testimony, they are shocked at all that it took to get to where I am today. But I had to be sold out in order to reach this level. I remember my sophomore year in high school. I joined the football team for the first time and the first goal I had was becoming a starter. I knew from the first day of 2 a day practices that it was going to take all that I had in order to start. So, I determined in my mind that I was going to give it 110% effort. It paid off and for the first year of my football career I was a starter.

There are several reasons why people are not sold out for their success. I will outline some of them over the next few chapters.

CHAPTER 4

Worthwhile goals

Is there something you've always wanted to do?
Something you need to do before you die.
When was the last time you made any steps at accomplishing it? If you can't remember the last time you did anything for that goal, don't worry. You're not any different than most people out there. But you should know that you deserve more.

God doesn't want you to be just another face in the mass of people on this planet.

The masses are not sold out because they don't have any worthwhile goals to accomplish. Worthwhile goals are like the nitro that they put in the cars from "The Fast and the Furious."

"Setting goals is the first step in turning the invisible into the visible."- Tony Robbins

They give us the instant boost that we need to reach the finish line. Goals are defined as the object of a person's ambition or effort; an aim or desired result. So many are moving aimlessly because they have nothing to attain or look forward to. A life without goals can lead to complacency, boredom, and lethargy.

You might ask, why are there a lot of people who have goals but fail to reach them?

I believe the answer lies in how worthwhile the goal is. If your goal doesn't ignite passion and a burning desire, there is a good chance that you won't be passionate enough to put in the groundwork.

Are your goals worthwhile? Do they get you excited to get up in the morning? If they do, then they are definitely worthwhile.

How can you tell?

The masses aren't sold out for success because they have no perspective of the future. If you live for just today you don't realize how the choices you make can influence you and your family 10, 15, and 20 years from now.

CHAPTER 5

Success Leaves Clues

I often think of Sherlock Holmes in regard to chasing dreams, attaining goals, and seeking success in a particular area. When Sherlock Holmes was given a problem, it was usually because no one else in London could solve it.

In other words, he was given impossible things to take care of. Whenever he set out to solve a mystery, he would rely on his own experience, his own genius to get things done. He couldn't rely on anyone else, except for maybe Mr. Watson, but even then, his trust only went so far.

For Sherlock Holmes, the only person he could really trust to get things done his way, was himself.

Because of this, the odds were highly in his favor. He rarely ever couldn't solve a case.

Unlike Sherlock Holmes, however, we don't have the ability to trust in ourselves to get to our goals and our dreams. Finding the kind of focus and attention required to reach out and grab them is nearly impossible to find.

Unless we have someone to help show us the way.

Everyone in life needs some sort of guide that they can follow on the journey. Nevertheless, you have the freedom to pick up your boots and go at the journey alone. But how much energy could you save if you had some type of mentor to follow that has been where you want to go.

I wasn't telling you the whole story with Sherlock Holmes, at least not exactly. You see, other than his life experience, he had another mentor. And that mentor wasn't from a source he would have expected.

It wasn't from a renowned professor from Oxford University, and it wasn't a crime investigator that had lots more experience than he did.

You see, the mentorship Mr. Holmes needed was in staying grounded.

He had such a high opinion of himself and his abilities, that he needed someone to show him how to be down to earth … how to be humble. And that mentor came in the form of his colleague and good friend, Dr. Watson. Without Watson's calming and steady influence, while Holmes would have remained a genius, he never would have achieved the heights he reached while with his friend.

He would have had no one to warn him when he was being over-confident or brash. He would have had no one to tell him to take a moment for himself when he was overwhelmed with a particular mystery. He needed the strong stillness of Watson to keep things real.

Just like Watson was for Holmes, a good mentor for you would be able to warn you of impending storms, like a weatherman. They can show you what worked for them and what didn't. Having a guide to pattern yourself after does 3 major things: saves you (1) time, (2) removes potential stress, and (3) boosts your energy. If we study the word of God it's evident that the Apostles had the greatest mentor, Jesus Christ. They served Him for 3 years as He taught them, mentored them, paved the way, and shared His life with them.

When his disciples were unsure how to cast demons out of wayward souls, or heal the sick and afflicted, Christ was there. He showed them how to heal, how to have faith, and how to invoke the power of heaven to call down miracles.

Without Jesus as a mentor, His disciples would never have been able to take His mantle after he left this earth. He was a guide in every sense of the word.

Likewise, with us, we MUST have a guide to get us to our dreams. A guide will save you all kinds of things.

1. Time – time you would otherwise spend learning to get your goals done.

After Christ was crucified, his disciples went back to their old lives. Some of them were tax collectors, some of them were carpenters. Many of them were fishermen.

Peter, James, and John were fishing one day, not long after Christ's crucifixion. They had been at the nets for most of the day, and they hadn't even smelled a fish. Needing to get some money, but not having any way to get their goal, they just continued fishing.

But they were ready to listen to anyone with a good idea.

So, when a man that looked and sounded familiar, but which they didn't recognize immediately, told them to put their nets on the other side of the boat – they listened. The result?

The nets go so full the ship nearly capsized. Was it not for the quick thinking of the captain of one of Peter's other fishing boats, they would have lost the record hall and their ship? After the nets were secured, Peter immediately recognized the newcomer as Jesus.

And Jesus had taught them an important lesson. First, follow His voice. Second, when you follow His voice, you will get things don't the right way.

A good mentor can save you years because of their lessons of how they failed in one area but overcame in another. I'm sorry to burst your bubble, but time is not on your side. Yesterday is gone and tomorrow doesn't exist yet.

Now is the time to seize the moment. The time to take action is now. Now is the time to write that book. Now is the time to start that business. Now is the time to go to school. Now is the time to get what you want in life. This book is a message to all age groups, all cultures, and people from all walks of life, especially for youths an adolescent. I can still remember my dad preaching to me when I was in my teens.

He would stress the fact that while I am young, I should finish school, graduate, take care of my business, watch out for all of the fast living and partying, and focus in on what I want to do in life. I remember him telling me that while I am taking care of my business, I should enjoy life at the same time. "Because after you graduate from grade school, the years seem to go by like a flash. And you know what?"

He was exactly right. I remember the years that I wasted in my early twenties. I remember the money and resources that I wasted from fast living and irresponsibility. But thankfully I can look back on those days, learn from them and help the next generation make the right choices to set themselves up for success.

Why Wait?

It is important to wait in life and be patient for some things like, the right spouse, the right house, and the right job. But do not wait with complacency. When we wait and are not active, we get lethargic and indifferent towards success. Inactivity leads to idleness, which leads to boredom, which leads to stagnation, which leads to mediocrity. Mediocrity is the biggest enemy to success.

"All good is hard. All evil is easy. Dying, losing, cheating, and mediocrity is easy. Stay away from easy." – Scott Alexander

The cure to conquering mediocrity is to set the bar high. An Olympic high jumper doesn't jump the same height as they did last year or the year before. They set the bar higher to reach greater breakthroughs and standards. So, reach for the stars, you never know what you might hit. Meet new clients, write more, step out of the box more, do what you've never done before.

What are you waiting for? Are you waiting for the pie in the sky? Guess what, it never comes. That pie in the sky doesn't exist. That pipe dream doesn't exist. It is a figment of your imagination if you haven't taken action. Dreams don't manifest for the inactive. So, seize the moment and go after what you want.

2. Stress – It can help you succeed and drive you to failure.

Jesus' disciples were at home on the water – at least the majority of them were. They were fishermen by professions, and most of their lives were spend in fishing boats. Yet it seemed that they were also more stressed out in boats than in any other environment.

They were always in storms.

They were always about to sink.

Fortunately, they had the Son of Man with them. So, whenever things got bleak, and they thought they were about to die, the Master would calm the seas. He would ease the cause of their stress, and the stress would dissipate – just like the torrid weather.

You can drive yourself crazy doing the same thing over and over. A mentor can show you a better way. It is amazing to me how many will refuse to follow a successful person because of pride and envy. Pride and being unteachable will cost you more precious time than you have.

During a particularly good sermon, Jesus appeared to be interrupted by a group of young children. They were messing around, having a good time, and being extremely distracting to those listening to Jesus preach. Incenses, they plead with the master to have the children shut up and go away.

His response was timeless:

"And he said, 'Truly, I say unto you, unless you turn and become like children, you will never enter into the kingdom of heaven." - Matthew 18:3

Jesus was clear to his disciples. Don't be prideful. Be willing to learn from those who know better than you. Don't think you know enough. If you end up trusting yourself more than Me, you will never get to heaven.

3. Energy booster – a mentor can give you energy you didn't know you had.

Another time Jesus' disciples were in the water. And there was yet another storm. They were toiling in their boat, and Christ was not with them. He had elected to stay behind so he could meditate. They, on the other hand, were toiling away at the boat for several hours.

Then they saw something.

It was something that scared the tar out of them.

A white figure what making its way across the see – and the waves were not letting up. They thought it was a ghost. If you thought they were already afraid, they were terrified when they thought they were seeing an undead spirit.

Christ called out to his disciples and let them know who he was.

In response, Peter called out to the Lord and besought him to let Peter walk on the water. Christ assented and Peter stepped onto the water. And then something crazy started to happen. Peter began to actually walk on the water.

I imagine it was something to behold.

But then Peter got scared. When he got scared, he started to sink. Still not quite to the Savior, he called out in desperation, "Lord, Save Me!" At the last moment, Christ put his hand into the water, grabbed a hold of Peter, and pulled him up. Then he smiled.

Instantly Peter and the crew breathed a collective sigh of relief.

They knew everything was going to be alright.

They will be able to encourage you and root you along the journey when you inevitably get stuck or in a rut. Think about it. If you were about to drive cross country would you leave your jumper cable at home or take them on the journey with you?

Know that if you do the same things that successful people do, you will get the same results. The key is not to skip or disregard the ingredients. If I were to buy a box of cake mix and fail to add the proper amount of sugar, milk, or eggs, it would not ok like what's on the box and the taste would be completely off. Even so, if you try to skip steps on your way to the journey, you miss opportunities to grow as well as mature. But if you keep your eyes open, you will see more opportunities to succeed …

… because Christ believes in you.

You see – you were born to succeed.

CHAPTER 6

You Were Born to Succeed

To overcome and succeed is within all of us. But to have success, action must take place. Sure, there will be set backs, valleys, and peaks, but consistent action outweighs them all. Every step you take up will get you closer and closer to the prize. I know by experience that once you succeed at one thing, it creates in you an insatiable appetite to do more and more. It creates in you a drive to do greater now then what you did last week. It creates a desire in you to try the impossible.

I can remember when I got the inspiration to write my first book, "Why am I Doing This?" I was so afraid but excited at the same time to be writing my own manuscript. I was so passionate about that project that it was all I could think about. I spent night and day thinking about it, pursuing it, and working on it until one day, it was finished and ready for release. It was at that moment that I came to the realization that

I was born for success. I know for a fact that I am born to do great things in life. But it comes at a price.

There were some sacrifices that had to be made. When others were watching television and playing video games, I was grinding. When others were snoring and dozing off, I was pushing the limits.

Do one thing every day that scares you."-Anonymous

I remember one day going to the gym. As I walked through the front door, I noticed a large gathering of people in the parking lot to my left. I proceeded to the front desk and asked the attendant what type of event was going on. The informed me that the Ironman contest was taking place outside of their facility. I said to myself right then and there that I would give it a try. If I failed and embarrassed myself, oh well, at least I went for it. So, I walked back to the parking lot where all the commotion and hoopla was going on. Boy did bite off more than I could chew. I was thinking maybe I was going to have to do some push-ups or maybe run a half mile or so. Turns out they had an all-out obstacle course that you had to complete in order to be considered an Ironman.

By the time I had finished the course, my shins and knees were burning. I had to sit down and catch my breath for more than a few minutes. I had actually participated in the event and completed it. The feeling was quiet confidence.

The desire to do better in life is ingrained in all of us. Mankind was meant to progress, grow, and do better than the generations before him. Why do you think the economy has gotten better over the centuries? We were once in an agrarian age where we farmed and hunted for everything. Then we loved on to the Industrial Age where we progressed and began to use railroads, steel mills, and assembly lines for everything. Now we are in the Information Age where knowledge moves at the speed of light. What's important today becomes obsolete tomorrow.

But remember that even though knowledge and information come and go, principles do not. Whatever age we are in, the same principles apply for success and progression to manifest. The methods to get there might change but the principles do not. Say for instance I get up in the morning and I decide I want my breakfast to consist of steak and scrambled eggs. One hundred years ago I would have to go slaughter the cow myself, gather the eggs out of the chicken coup, and prepare the meal in the comforts of my home on a gas skillet. Now I can go online, choose my favorite grocery store, and have them deliver the same food to my doorstep for a minimal fee. I am still required to cook the food in the comforts of my home. (Unless I have a maid) But notice that no one gathered the food, ordered it online, or made it for me. I still had to follow the principle to take action.

CHAPTER 7

Success feels good

Success feels good. It feels good to start something and finish it. The fulfillment of an accomplishment can't be compared to any other feeling. Honestly, I believe that our emotional state is connected to how we conquer certain mountains in life. There is a fool proof way to set goals and achieve them on a regular basis. I like to call it living in reality.

This means that you set goals that are reasonable, achievable, and connected to what your values really are. I believe that the reason we sometimes don't accomplish a goal is because it is what we think we want when in reality it really isn't. For example, we might tell ourselves that in a year or so we will set a goal to start a business and bring in an income of $100,000 a year. But we never stop and ask ourselves why we desire that much, what it will take, and if starting a business is part of our goals and values.

So, there are no specifics involved in this process. A better way to analyze this goal is to write it down and see if this aligns with our values. It would look something like this:

My values:

> God
> Family
> Financial freedom

So, the next thing to do is to see how a business and extra income would align to these values.

1. With extra income I could honor God by giving and sowing financial seeds in the form of tithes, offerings, and building funds.

2. My family and I could take more vacations and have discretionary income for luxury items and investments for the future.

3. I could be financially free by having the business and its systems run themselves in due time.

Just by listing our values and lining them with our potential goals will shed a light on where we need to go and what we need to commit our time and resources towards. Doing so would save lots of time and heartache.

I have found that writing my own personal mission and vision statements have had a profound effect on my life.

"My mission in life is not merely to survive, but to thrive." Maya Angelou

I love what the late guru Stephen Covey has to say about mission and vision statements.

"A mission statement is not something you write overnight, but fundamentally, your mission statement becomes your constitution, the solid expression of your vision and values. It becomes the criterion by which you measure everything else in your life." Stephen Covey

Do you realize that countries, nations, kingdoms, and corporations all have mission statements? So why not have a mission and vision statement for yourself? Why not have one for your family? They would provide you with a sense of direction and freedom. Freedom in the sense that you are not shackled by aimlessness.

Let's look at a few mission statements, vision statements, and constitutions that are prevalent in our society. Chick-fil-A has a very powerful mission and vision.

"To glorify God by being a faithful steward of all that is entrusted to us and to have a positive influence on all who come into contact with Chick-fil-A."

Now anyone who has visited a Chick-fil-a restaurant lately clearly knows why they stay busy and the lines are always out of the door and around the corner. They glorify God by being closed on Sundays in observance of those who would like to worship or go to church on that day. They hire employees who are customer service oriented, work hard, and believe in the company's vision and beliefs. They treat their customers with honor, respect, and keep tidy restaurants. There is a great atmosphere when you eat in their locations and they go out of their way to cater to your children. This is all established and guided by their values which are aligned within their mission and vision.

Having an awareness of our core values and mission will help us be better people, parents, stewards, owners, and employees. So, let's look at some common core values that we have:

Loyalty

Loyalty is a strong feeling of support or allegiance to a person or thing. It's a feeling you get towards someone or something, when someone or something that is appealing to you comes your way, and you decide to go with the person or thing you had originally.

This value is important to have because it allows you to be intent in following and do the things the person or thing you are loyal to expect of you. When you are loyal to your family, you choose activities that revolve around them, instead of around other things.

Honesty

Honest is just a fancy way to say tell the truth. You can develop it by practice. And if you're going to succeed in life, it's something that will help distinguish you from everyone else. Especially in the dishonest world we are living in right now.

Commitment

Commitment is the state or quality of being dedicated to a cause or activity. It is a lot like loyalty, but different for one very important reason. A commitment is an obligation or promise to do something – like being loyal.

It's something that you need to have in your life if you want to achieve success. You need to be committed to Christ, and you need to be committed to your goals.

Strong work ethic

A strong work ethic is more than just a desire to work had and work diligently. It's a way to live your life. When you have a strong work ethic, it bleeds over into all you do. It's not always easy to develop and can really only get stronger as you practice it more.

Faithfulness

Faithfulness is a great quality to develop. It involves feelings like loyalty, fidelity, constancy, and devotion. If you are faithful you will be true to your beliefs and your convictions. You will be dedicated to your work and your beliefs, even when things get tough. With it you can move mountains, and without it you can get blown away by the faintest breeze.

Security

If security is one of your core values, your actions will place emphasis on creating a life that is secure. Creating a life where you can have predicted outcomes, where you can have a set of rules of the road to fall back on when you enter a new phase of life that is unfamiliar to you.

I feel that these core values can impact us positively, and you have them, they will make you a better, more well-rounded person. However, not all core values are positive. It is possible for us to have some core values that can hinder and diminish the power we can have in life, such as some of these.

Deception

When deception is one of your core values, you aren't necessarily trying to deceive people all day, every day. You may even do what's right from time to time. However, as a core value, deception will be something you rely on to get what you want or need out of life.

You may not be telling outright lies, but you won't be telling the whole truth either. But that won't matter, as you will be moving forwards towards your goals, whatever the cost. This is an expensive way to live, as you will find yourself worn out from continuing to use people for your own prosperity. Better to go the route of honesty and commitment.

Lying

Lying takes deception to another level. While all forms of lying are a form of deception, not all deceptions are a form of lying. Lying involves telling other something that is just not true, period. If lying is one of your core values, while you may work hard, and be seriously loyal to family, friends, or business partners, you will not value the truth.

You will use lies and deceptions to get what you want, without thinking thoroughly about the impact you will have on the lives of others. The short-term result may net you a positive gain, but the long-term result will be the loss of your reputation, your relationship, and your integrity.

Using others

When you use others, you place the value of other human beings below the value of getting what you want. Think of David and Uriah in the Old Testament.

David wanted to marry Bath Sheba, after he saw her bathing on her roof. In order to get to her, he ordered Uriah, her husband, to be sent to the front lines, where he was ultimately killed in battle. While this is not the same result that you will see when you use others, the price you put on their worth, whether great or small, will tell them a lot about who you are as a person.

And believe me, it won't be a good thing.

Sexual promiscuity

This is a core value that people bring into their relationships. Not being faithful to your spouse or partner not only breeds contempt and distrust, but it creates a pattern of unfaithfulness that can and will bleed into every aspect of your life.

Luxury in excess

This core value is something that not everyone agrees on. If you're successful, and you're able to "win" the game of money, some people say they should be able to enjoy their wealth. Others say they should share it. The decision is up to you. Just make sure you know what your definition of success is, and how your luxuries put you with your relationship with God.

CHAPTER 8

Total Life Success

Success should infiltrate your entire life. I'm talking about success in your finances, marriage, singleness, relationships, job, business, and the rest. But it will take a high level of effort on your part. We were put on this earth to succeed. As a matter of fact, the Bible says that God desires that we should have "good success"

"This Book of the Law shall not depart from your mouth, but you[c] shall meditate in it day and night, that you may observe to do according to all that is written in it. For then you will make your way prosperous, and then you will have **good success**. 9 Have I not commanded you? Be strong and of good courage; do not be afraid, nor be dismayed, for the Lord your God is with you wherever you go."—Joshua 1:8-9

So, are you currently enjoying life? You deserve success. You deserve to live the good life. There is a divine pattern designed for us to live the good life through Jesus Christ. I have searched the scriptures and outlined the lives of many Bible heroes and their daily habits that led to success and victory in every aspect of life. In the next few chapters, I have fashioned some key attributes of those who have lived a dynamic life for Christ.

PART II

CHAPTER 9

Eternal Success

You can have success from a worldly perspective and even enjoy it for a season. But what about the type of success that has eternal ramifications? What about the type of success that lasts for a lifetime, and then some?

Many today have this scripture misconstrued and backwards. They are seeking the things and leaving the kingdom and God's righteousness at the back burner. I have come to find out that Jesus preached against worry in these preceding verses because worry, doubt, and a lack of faith are what keeps us from seeking first the kingdom of God. We are worried about everything under the sun from our bills, to our kids, to our pets, and everything else that God has promised He would take care of.

So, it comes down to who and what we are trusting to bring us success. I'm not saying you shouldn't work, have fun, or seek for better in life. The trouble comes when this becomes our sole ambition and causes us to disregard the will of God for us. When was the last time you shared your faith with someone?

When was the last time you spent time with the Lord to see what He wants versus what you want?

On another note...

Many want success for their children and ignore their own relationship with the Lord. Time goes on and they look up and they haven't accomplished anything significant in life. I'm not saying that we shouldn't do right by our children, but you don't want to use them as a cloak to escape from what God has for you in life. I have had friends and associates work from sunup to sundown to get good things for their children, and by the age of 40 or 50 they haven't done anything for themselves.

CHAPTER 10

Keys to living a Dynamic Life for Christ

"The 2 Things in Life that you never have to apologize for are Success and Favor"-Dr. E.O.M III

Many wonder why two people in the same community of faith can live such radically different lives. It has nothing to do with background, ethnicity, titles, or economics. It has to do with simple everyday habits and choices that the individual makes. There is such great power in choice. You can choose to wake up, get out of bed, brush your teeth, and take a bath. Or you can choose to sleep all day, have halitosis, and stink up the room. You can choose to live the life in Christ that "eyes have not seen" or you can settle for less than the best that God has for you. The choice is yours!! Does God prefer one believer over another?

Acts 10:34

"Then Peter opened his mouth, and said, of a truth I perceive that God is no respecter of persons..."

I think not. Does God say, "I'm going to cause this child of mine to fail in life and cause this one to have great success?"

"And he said to him, 'Son, you have always been with me, and all that is mine is yours. But we had to celebrate and rejoice, for this brother of yours was dead and has begun to live and was lost and has been found.'"-Luke 15:31-32

I don't think so.

Or maybe it's the enemies' fault that we live mediocre lives when God wants the best for us...

"Submit therefore to God. Resist the devil and he will flee from you. Draw near to God and He will draw near to you. Cleanse your hands, you sinners; and purify your hearts, you double-minded." -James 4:7-8

Hmm. I'm still not convinced...

There are always principles in life rather saved or unsaved that must be followed in order for anyone to survive and thrive. As with the natural, so with the spiritual. There is a world beyond our comprehension that eyes have not seen, nor ears heard. There is a war going on behind the scenes and much is at stake. We are going to have to decide to live a life that is pleasing to the Lord, or go on with a meager, beggars like existence. Children of a King do not live beggarly lives. Children of Kings live lives that most can only imagine. That life is available to us right now if we would reach out and seize it by faith. It's going to take every ounce of energy you have to take it by force.

If we take time to search out the scriptures, we can unlock the keys and principles that are vital to living a dynamic life for Christ.

CHAPTER 11

Jesus the Prayer Champion

Jesus was a prayer addict. It's in prayer that He found strength from the Father. It's in prayer that He found direction for the next day's work. It's in prayer that He found rest. If Jesus spent so much time in prayer, how much more should His followers have saturated themselves in prayer?

Matthew 14:23

"After He had sent the crowds away, He went up on the mountain by Himself to pray; and when it was evening, He was there alone."

Luke 6:12

"It was at this time that He went off to the mountain to pray, and He spent the whole night in prayer to God."

Jesus spent an ample amount of time in prayer to God. He wasn't praying patty cake prayers neither. The Bible says that He "offered up both prayers and supplications with loud crying and tears to the One able to save Him from death, and He was heard because of His piety." So, it takes fiery prayer to live the dynamic Christian life. The Bible says that the "effective fervent prayer of the righteous availeth much!!" In prayer God will release:

1. Revelation
2. Ideas
3. Solutions
4. Perspective

It is my belief that many believers live shallow and unfulfilled lives because they have shallow prayer lives. Many wonders why they don't see healing's, miracles, and wonders taking place in their lives. They wonder why their emotions are constantly getting the best of them. One day they are happy, the next hour they are down in the dumps. If they would only take Jesus' advice and "pray for an hour" they would see God do amazing things through them. I guess the old saying is true, "Much prayer, much power, little prayer, little power."

God wants to give the believer power to advance against the enemy. But without prayer, you have no defense against him. Without prayer you end up living the defeated life versus the dynamic life of Christ. The enemy knows that the believer who doesn't pray is an easy target for his imps. I say imps because they are the first line of his defense. He doesn't have to dispatch his powers and authorities because a prayerless believer is light work for him.

Oh, but the believer that prays fervently can see right through the enemy's tactics. They know how to infiltrate his territory and take back everything that he stole from them. It's comical that many don't live the dynamic life because they fail to realize they have an enemy that has stolen something from them. The enemy comes to steal, kill, and destroy. He wants to take your joy, money, health, and everything else God has freely given for our enjoyment.

With fiery prayer you can take back anything and everything that he has stolen. Your victory is in prayer. Your future is in prayer. Your anointing is released in prayer. Prayer, prayer, prayer, and more prayer are what's needful.

I have personally received so much in prayer. Business plans, prophecy from the Lord, what type of vehicle to buy, debt reduction strategies, how, who, and when to give my tithes and offerings, and so much more.

Will you build an altar for the Lord? Abram built altars to the Lord and sought His face every time God expanded him and brought him to a new destination in life. Every time Abram built an altar and sought the Lord, He revealed to Abram his next journey, destination, plans, and discoveries. It is in prayer where God told Abram that he is giving him a new name, Abraham. Could it be that the reason many in the Body haven't received direction, instructions, and details about life is because they are not praying? Could it be that the reason we see so much corruption going on in government and high places is because of a lack of strong prayer? Could it be that the reason we see principalities taking over neighborhoods, districts, wards, cities, and nations is because of a lack of prayer by believers? God said that He is looking for one man to stand in the gap and make up the hedge…

And I sought for a man among them that should make up the hedge, and stand in the gap before me for the land, that I should not destroy it: but I found none. – Ezekiel 22:30

I promise you if believers everywhere would get into prayer God would heal the land and in return, He would heal broken lives, misfortune in our homes, and restore us to living dynamic lives for the Kingdom!! Whatever you need is in prayer. Ask and you shall receive, seek and you shall find, knock and the door will be open to you. It's in the asking that God hears us. It's in the seeking that God motives us. It's in the knocking that gets God to open up doors that no man can shut. We have to develop the attitude of the persistent widow. We have to bug and bother God.

Now, He was always telling them a parable to show that they ought to pray and not to lose heart, saying:

"In a certain city there was a judge who did not fear God and did not respect man. 3 There was a widow in that city, and she kept coming to him, saying, 'Give me legal protection from my opponent.' 4 For a while he was unwilling; but afterward he said to himself, 'Even though I do not fear God nor respect man, 5 yet because this widow bothers me, I will give her legal protection, otherwise by continually coming she will wear me out.'" And the Lord said, "Hear what the unrighteous judge *said; 7 now, will not God bring about justice for His elect who cry to Him day and night, and will He delay long over them? 8 I tell you that He will bring about justice for them quickly. However, when the Son of Man comes, will He find faith on the earth?"-Luke 18:1-8

God will not delay in answering your prayers people of God. But it's time to get in the game of prayer and take part in God's plans for the earth.

Here are some reasons from the scriptures that people don't pray:

1. Lack of training

Are you blind to the fact that like anything else in life you need proper training? To be a firefighter in the natural realm you have to go to school. The same applies for doctors, lawyers, teachers, etc. You have to take a prayer 101 course to learn the art of praying.

It happened that while Jesus was praying in a certain place, after He had finished, one of His disciples said to Him, "Lord, teach us to pray just as John also taught his disciples."-Luke 11:1

So, if John the Baptist taught his disciples how to pray, and Jesus the same, shouldn't we seek out training on how to pray? I God for my spiritual leaders who taught us how to pray properly. As a result, I am living the dynamic life I've always dreamed of. It is a blessing to be able to partake with God as an agent of prayer. Angels will meet you at your house if you simply would take time to pray. Angels would be released on your behalf that will touch your friends and family members. God will begin to rebuke the enemy and his agents in order that answers may come to you.

2. Lose heart

Losing heart deals with giving up before you see the manifestation of answered prayer.

"Men ought to always pray, and not lose heart"

It's time to get back into position as watchman on the wall. When we get tired, faint hearted and off our posts, the enemy has access to rob us of God's goodness. Don't lose heart.

3. Wrong motives

"Ye ask, and receive not, because ye ask amiss, that ye may consume it upon your lusts." - James 4:3

It's time to hit the bull's eye in prayer. I am convinced that some do not receive – not because of a lack of prayer - but because of impure motives when they pray.

"God cannot be mocked…"

If you pray with wrong intentions, God will hear your prayers, but they will go in one ear and out of the other.

Moreover, as for me, far be it from me that I should sin against the Lord by ceasing to pray for you; but I will instruct you in the good and right way. -1 Samuel 12:23

It's a sin not to pray!!

CHAPTER 12

Daniel the Leader on Fasting

Fasting is almost a lost art in the Christian world today. The word fast comes from the Hebrew word sum. It also comes from the Greek word nesteia. It means to abstain from food. So, in its original meaning, to fast is to give up food or turn your plate upside down for a period of time.

It is my belief that many in the Body of Christ today do not fast because they have no earthly idea why they should be fasting. Some believe that fasting is Justine ancient ritual that monks and priests do as a religious duty. Still some believe that fasting is just to lose weight. These are some wild misconceptions that need to be straightened out and discussed at length. Why would God encourage us to give up food when He tells us that He has "given us all things richly to enjoy?"

Fasting and our motives for fasting are really what God is paying attention to. If you starve yourself but your heart isn't right or your motives are wrong, God will not be moved on your behalf. So, let's see what scripture has to say about true fasting and the type of fasting that is acceptable and unacceptable to God.

> "In fact, in the day of your fast you find pleasure,
> And exploit all your laborers.
> Indeed, you fast for strife and debate,
> And to strike with the fist of wickedness.
> You will not fast as you do this day,
> To make your voice heard on high." - Isaiah 58:3-4

The first thing wrong with this type of fasting is that there was no compassion being shown as a result of their sacrifice. They were exploiting their laborers during this concentration. A true Biblical fast will cause you to develop compassion and "love thy neighbor as thyself."

The next thing we see is that these same people were committing the works of the flesh. They were given to strife, contention, and unnecessary debating amongst one another. In other words, they were debating just to be heard and "one up" someone else.

> So, what type of fast does God requires? Verses 6-7 say:
> "Is this not the fast that I have chosen:
> To lose the bonds of wickedness,
> To undo the [c]heavy burdens,
> To let the oppressed, go free,
> And that you break every yoke
> Is it not to share your bread with the hungry?
> And that you bring to your house the poor who are [d] cast out;

When you see the naked, that you cover him,
And not hide yourself from your own flesh?"

There is a fast that we can choose, and there is a fast that God has chosen. His way is always better than our limited perspective. His way of fasting causes us to utterly break the back of wickedness that has attached itself to us, our families, our neighborhoods, churches, and country. His way of fasting ushers in freedom from shackles, chains, and heavy burdens. His way of fasting gives us a heart for the poor, the hungry, the afflicted, and the outcasts.

Fasting is not abstaining from social media for a time period. That would be more of a discipline. Fasting." specifically as it relates to the Bible is to give up food for a period of time in order to focus on what God is saying and doing. Trust me when I say that giving up food for a long period of time will help you to appreciate what God has placed on your dinner table. It will help you to have compassion on those who don't have it as good as you. Maybe the reason we see so many hungry souls on the street is because there is a lack of proper fasting today.

There are a couple of reasons I have identified why there is a lack of fasting today. If you pick up your Bible and read from Genesis to Revelation in a year, you will clearly see that the great heroes of the Word had a sound fasting ministry. Let's take a moment to look at Daniel and the way he fasted.

"But Daniel resolved that he would not defile himself with the royal rations of food and wine; so, he asked the palace master to allow him not to defile himself. Now God allowed Daniel to receive favor and compassion from the palace master.

The palace master said to Daniel, "I am afraid of my lord the king; he has appointed your food and your drink. If he should see you in poorer condition than the other young men of your own age, you would endanger my head with the king." Then Daniel asked the guard whom the palace master had appointed over Daniel, Hananiah, Mishael, and Azariah: "Please test your servants for ten days. Let us be given vegetables to eat and water to drink. You can then compare our appearance with the appearance of the young men who eat the royal rations, and deal with your servants according to what you observe." So, he agreed to this proposal and tested them for ten days. At the end of ten days it was observed that they appeared better and fatter than all the young men who had been eating the royal rations. So, the guard continued to withdraw their royal rations and the wine they were to drink, and gave them vegetables. To these four young men God gave knowledge and skill in every aspect of literature and wisdom; Daniel also had insight into all visions and dreams." - Daniel 1:8-17

The first key we should notice is that Daniel desired to fast because he didn't want to identify himself with the customs of the pagan nation, he dwelt in. The food that the Babylonians ate at that time would first be sacrificed to their idol gods and placed before the people to eat. For Daniel to continue to eat this type of food would be a conviction to him. Fasting, if done properly, will clean us out of all that may defile us. Rather it be impure thoughts, habits, rituals, mindsets, etc.

The second thing we see is that through this fast, God gave Daniel "favor and compassion" with the palace master. The palace master was willing to risk his very life in order to accommodate Daniel. Could it be that the reason we don't see the favor of the Lord moving in our lives is because there is a lack of fasting?

Third, we see that the overall health of Daniel and his 3 friends was much better than those who had eaten the defiled foods. So not only does fasting present spiritual benefits, but there are natural benefits that come as well. And finally, through this fast, God release an abundance of knowledge and skill to these 4 young men.

There is another important barrier to fasting that I want to discuss. We like to call it the "belly god."

"Their end is destruction; their god is the belly; and their glory is in their shame; their minds are set on earthly things. But our citizenship is in heaven, and it is from there that we are expecting a Savior, the Lord Jesus Christ." - Philippians 3:19-20

There is a god that we can serve as believers that gets precedence over the true and living God. Simply put, there is a lack of fasting going on today because we love to eat.

CHAPTER 13

Are you devoted to the word like the first church?

"They devoted themselves to the APOSTLES TEACHING and to fellowship, to the breaking of bread and to prayer." - Acts 2:42

Herein lies a major key that believers today either miss it, or the know but disregard it. Some say the Bible is outdated, antiquated, and not relevant for today's culture.

Poor miss guided souls!!

There are kinds that are not transformed but stagnated and distorted in their thinking, simply because they fail to read and search the scriptures. Some feel the word of God is boring and difficult. Some feel they don't have time to read it. I have come to find out that in life we all have choices. You can choose what you make time for. There is no way that you are too busy in a 24-hour day to spend 15 minutes reading and basking in God's Holy Word.

Maybe we are afraid because the word of God is Holy. Maybe we are afraid to read it because we fear that the scriptures will come alive and force us to get ungodly living out of our lives. Maybe we are afraid that if we read, we would have to lay down the beer bottle, which will improve our health. Maybe we fear we have to stop sleeping around, which would please God and sanctify our bodies. Or maybe we would be convicted of our selfishness and have to slowly become selfless.

There are a countless number of reasons why believers don't read the Bible. It's unfortunate, because God guarantees some major blessings, successes, and breakthroughs for the Bible thumper. Let's take a look at a few.

"But whose delight is in the law of the Lord, and who meditates on his Law Day and night. That person is like a tree planted by streams of water, which yields its fruit in season and whose leaf does not wither— whatever they do prospers." - Psalm 1:2-3

In these two verses, God has laid down promises for those who delight in His word. If you delight in something, then it should give to great joy and gladness. We should be hungry and eager to read the word. This verse shows us that if we read and meditate on His word, He will cause us to be planted and stable. An oak tree that is planted and stable is unmovable. The winds and storms may come, but it still remains planted and steady in the same place. Not only will we be planted but we will be planted by streams of living eater which is the source of life for any tree. Life, growth, and cultivation will be continually received by the one who stays rooted in the word of God. In addition to being planted we will yield fruit in due season. The problem with some of us is that we are impatient with God and His word. We want overnight success and He doesn't always work like that. Fruit takes time to grow and be cultivated. If we read the Word, we are likened to a stable tree that is yielding fruits of righteousness, holiness, goodness, mercy, and so on.

But the fruit of the Spirit is love, joy, peace, forbearance, kindness, goodness, faithfulness, gentleness and self-control. Against such things there is no law. -Galatians 5:22-23

CHAPTER 14

Giving like Solomon

Have you practiced the art of giving as it relates to living a successful life in Christ?
Let me repeat this.
Have you practiced the art of giving as it relates to living a successful life in Christ?

Being a giver in our walk with the Lord will make us successful in due time. Most of the great heroes of the Bible were givers. Look at Abraham, Isaac, Jacob, and the Macedonians. The Bible says that Abraham was a faithful tither even before the law was received by the Israelites.

"Then Melchizedek king of Salem brought out bread and wine. He was priest of God Most High, and he blessed Abram, saying, "Blessed be Abram by God Most High, Creator of heaven and earth. And praise be to God Most High, who delivered your enemies into your hand." Then Abram gave him a tenth of everything." - Genesis 14:18-20

So, God gave Abraham victory in the preceding battle. In fact, God have Abraham the victory over five major kings of that time. Then God sent His priest, Melchizedek to speak a major blessing over Abraham. Did Abraham say, "Thank you God" or "I appreciate you Pastor?"

No, Abraham sowed tithes of everything that he had to God and the man of God. Even today, some believers miss or disregard giving a blessing to their shepherds and those who teach and preach the Word of the Lord. What a shame and what a major way to cause our blessings and successes to be missed.

It's vital that we as a people get back to being faithful in our giving and sowing to the work of the Lord. Without sowing there is no reciprocation. Without sowing there is no growth. Imagine a field full of fertile dirt. If no one takes the time to sow any seeds into it, no harvests will ever manifest.

Isaac was a sacrificial sower and followed in the same pattern of his father Abraham. The Bible says that in the same year he reaped a one hundredfold blessing. But we will discuss his sacrifices in a later chapter - so stay tuned. Even Jacob, who was Isaacs's son, was a faithful tither like his grandfather, Abraham. These next verses will show you the major promises that God gave to Jacob because of his seeds.

Then Jacob made a vow, saying, "If God will be with me and will watch over me on this journey I am taking and will give me food to eat and clothes to wear so that I return safely to my father's household, then the Lord will be my God and this stone that I have set up as a pillar will be God's house, and of all that you give me I will give you a tenth." - Genesis 28:20-22

So, because of tithing, God gave Jacob His presence. God also promised He would watch over Jacob, give him provision, clothing, and a safe journey back home. This sounds like major success to me.

I haven't forgotten about the radical giving of King Solomon. I wanted to paint the picture of the many who were givers before he was. The Bible says,

"Now the king went to Gibeon to sacrifice there, for that was the great high place: Solomon offered a thousand burnt offerings on that altar. At Gibeon the Lord appeared to Solomon in a dream by night; and God said, "Ask! What shall I give you?"

"And Solomon said: "You have shown great mercy to your servant David my father, because he walked before you in truth, in righteousness, and in uprightness of heart with you; you have continued this great kindness for him, and you have given him a son to sit on his throne, as it is this day. Now, O Lord my God, you have made your servant king instead of my father David, but I am a little child; I do not know how to go out or come in. And your servant is in the midst of your people whom you have chosen, a great people, too numerous to be numbered or counted. Therefore, give to your servant an understanding heart to judge your people that I may discern between good and evil. For who is able to judge this great people of yours?"

"The speech pleased the Lord, that Solomon had asked this thing. Then God said to him: "Because you have asked this thing, and have not asked long life for yourself, nor have asked riches for yourself, nor have asked the life of your enemies, but have asked for yourself understanding to discern justice, behold, I have done according to your words; see, I have given you a wise and understanding heart, so that there has not been anyone like you before you, nor shall any like you arise after you. And I have also given you what you have not asked: both riches and honor, so that there shall not be anyone like you among the kings all your days. So if you walk in My ways, to keep My statutes and My commandments, as your father David walked, then I will lengthen[c] your days."

"Then Solomon awoke; and indeed, it had been a dream. And he came to Jerusalem and stood before the ark of the covenant of the Lord, offered up burnt offerings, offered peace offerings, and made a feast for all his servants." - 1 Kings 3:4-15.

CHAPTER 15

Mercy, Mercy Me

To live the Dynamic life in Christ, you have to practice the art of mercy. Actually, mercy is a gift listed in Romans 12:8. It says, "He who exhorts, in his exhortation; he who gives, with liberality; he who leads, with diligence; he who shows mercy, with cheerfulness. In the Greek, mercy comes from the word eleos, and it means kindness or good will towards the miserable and the afflicted, joined with a desire to help them.

So, do you have a desire to help those who are in need with your time, talents, skills, and abilities? Do you have a passion to see others be empowered and out of poverty? Do you see the suffering and lack of others as a problem or just another day in the park?

You would be surprised at how many of us go through the day and ignore the hurting and pain that others are going through. Mercy will ignite you to give to those in need as well as share the gospel of Jesus Christ with them. Not only do the poor and afflicted need tangible items, but they need the gospel of Jesus to save them and give them a durable hope.

CHAPTER 16

Success-Imagine That!!

What can you imagine for yourself?
Imagination is described as the faculty or action of forming new ideas, or images or concepts of external objects not present to the senses. What can you imagine for yourself? What great lengths, heights, and depths do you want to achieve? Are you satisfied with low hanging fruits? Can you see greater things for yourself and your family? Sometimes all you can do is use your imagination to put you into the world of your dreams.

Take Jacob, our forefather for instance. He was in dire circumstances - working for an uncle who tricked him into working 14 years instead 7. On top of that, his uncle constantly changed his wages. One year, Jacob was making minimum wage, the next he was making less. He might get a small bonus this year, next year the bonus would be taxed!! One thing after another. It was like he was the hamster on the wheel just running and running and running.

He eventually said enough is enough. The Bible says, "And you know that with all my might I have served your father. Yet your father has deceived me and changed my wages ten times, but God did not allow him to hurt me." - Genesis 31:6-7"

After so much turmoil, Jacob imagined greater in life and began to receive divine ideas to be acted on. His imagination coupled with obedience and divine ideas made him wealthy beyond his dreams.

"Now Jacob took for himself rods of green poplar and of the almond and chestnut trees, peeled white strips in them, and exposed the white which was in the rods. And the rods which he had peeled, he set before the flocks in the gutters, in the watering troughs where the flocks came to drink, so that they should conceive when they came to drink. So, the flocks conceived before the rods, and the flocks brought forth streaked, speckled, and spotted. Then Jacob separated the lambs and made the flocks face toward the streaked and all the brown in the flock of Laban; but he put his own flocks by themselves and did not put them with Laban's flock. And it came to pass, whenever the stronger livestock conceived, that Jacob placed the rods before the eyes of the livestock in the gutters that they might conceive among the rods. But when the flocks were feeble, he did not put them in; so, the feebler were Laban's and the stronger Jacob's. Thus, the man became exceedingly prosperous, and had large flocks, female and male servants, and camels and donkeys." - Genesis 30:37-43

CHAPTER 17

Success – Will you sacrifice your Isaac to go higher?

What are you willing to sacrifice to live a dynamic and successful life? Jesus said that He came to give us life, and that more abundantly. So, it is your divine right to have as much success as you can stand. But realize that there are always conditions. Take for instance the sacrifices of Abraham and Isaac. The Bible says in Genesis 22:1-2:

"And it came to pass after these things, that God did tempt Abraham, and said unto him, Abraham: and he said, Behold, here I am. And he said, take now thy son, thine only son Isaac, whom thou lovest, and get thee into the land of Moriah; and offer him there for a burnt offering upon one of the mountains which I will tell thee of."

So, picture this, God commanded Abraham to sacrifice the promised seed, Isaac. This was the same seed that God promised Abraham and Sarah they would have at an old age. So, the two of them had to exhibit great faith and patience for this promised seed to arrive. Then God turns around and tells them to sacrifice the child? Was God losing His mind? Maybe God had amnesia and forgot this was the promised seed?

Many of us today have our own Isaacs that we refuse to let go of. Our Isaac could be anything that we hold dear to our hearts and refuse to give up if called to. Your Isaac could be your car, clothes, time, money, friendships that need to be severed. Anything that you refuse to give up going up can be considered an Isaac.

I have had to sacrifice an Isaac myself in this walk. I had bought a beautiful luxury vehicle some years ago and God told me clearly to give it away. I struggled with it for a few days, but faith would not allow me to refuse God or say no.

When you give up your Isaac by faith, God shifts you, promotes, blesses you, quickens you, and places you on the fast track to great success.

Let's look at Abraham's response to Gods commands.

"And they came to the place which God had told him of; and Abraham built an altar there, and laid the wood in order, and bound Isaac his son, and laid him on the altar upon the wood. And Abraham stretched forth his hand and took the knife to slay his son. And the angel of the Lord called unto him out of heaven, and said, Abraham, Abraham: and he said, here am I."- Genesis 22:9-11

Abraham was willing and obedient to obey the Lords commandments. If only we as a community today had this same kind of faith and obedience, God would increase us in our finances and callings.

If we fast-track to the book of Hebrews, we can see Abraham's mindset about this whole event.

"By faith Abraham, when he was tested, offered up Isaac, and he who had received the promises was offering up his only begotten son; it was he to whom it was said, "In Isaac your descendants shall be called." He considered that God is able to raise people even from the dead, from which he also received him back as a type." - Hebrews 11:17-19

What great faith and perspective on the power of God and that which was to come! Sacrifice and giving up something in the short term is a way of life. In order to gain better health, you might have to give up gluttony, rich foods, cigarettes, or too much sugar. In order to finish reading that book you might have to put down the joystick or cut down on television time. Your level of willingness and obedience will determine your level of advancement.

"If ye be willing and obedient, ye shall eat the good of the land: But if ye refuse and rebel, ye shall be devoured with the sword: for the mouth of the Lord hath spoken it." - Isaiah 1:19-20

The rich young ruler missed out on the dynamic life. Look at his attitude.

"And someone came to Him and said, "Teacher, what good thing shall I do that I may obtain eternal life?" And He said to him, "Why are you asking Me about what is good? There is only One who is good; but if you wish to enter into life, keep the commandments." Then he *said to Him, "Which ones?" And Jesus said, "You shall not commit murder; You shall not commit adultery; You shall not steal; You shall not bear false witness; 19 Honor your father and mother; and You shall love your neighbor as yourself." The young man *said to Him, "All these things I have kept; what am I still lacking?" Jesus said to him, "If you wish to be complete, go and sell your possessions and give to the poor, and you will have treasure in heaven; and come, follow Me." But when the young man heard this statement, he went away grieving; for he was one who owned much property. And Jesus said to His disciples, "Truly I say to you, it is hard for a rich man to enter the kingdom of heaven. 24 Again I say to you, it is easier for a camel to go through the eye of a needle, than for a rich man to enter the kingdom of God." - Matthew 19:16-24

    His first problem was assuming that he had it all together and there was nothing left for him to accomplish. But he recognized that even though he had accomplished many things according to the world's standards that God's ways and His wisdom are higher than that of the world. He was rich, had authority, clout, and probably much more. But the one thing he loved, his possessions, he could let go to go higher in this life. It's unfortunate that there are some today in the church who love God and sincerely want to obey Him. But they're grip is too tight on that which they love the most.

    Esau missed out on the blessing and inheritance of his father Isaac. Esau's Isaac was food and his belly. He was so hungry that he sold his birthright for a bowl of stew.

    "Once when Jacob was cooking stew, Esau came in from the field, and he was exhausted. 30 And Esau said to Jacob, "Let me eat some of that red stew, for I am exhausted!" (Therefore, his name was called Edom. Jacob said, "Sell me your birthright now." Esau said, "I am about to die; of what use is a birthright to me?" 33 Jacob said, "Swear to me now." So, he swore to him and sold his birthright to Jacob. Then Jacob gave Esau bread and lentil stew, and he ate and drank and rose and went his way. Thus, Esau despised his birthright.? - Genesis 25:29-34

I want to encourage anyone reading this not to sell yourself short of your birthright, inheritance, and the blessings of the Lord.

CHAPTER 18

Fighters mentality

> "Then Caleb quieted the people before Moses, and said, "Let us go up at once and take possession, for we are well able to overcome it." But the men who had gone up with him said, "We are not able to go up against the people, for they are stronger than we." And they gave the children of Israel a bad report of the land which they had spied out, saying, "The land through which we have gone as spies is a land that devours its inhabitants, and all the people whom we saw in it are men of great stature. There we saw the giants (the descendants of Anak came from the giants); and we were like grasshoppers in our own sight, and so we were in their sight." - Numbers 13:30-33

You must have a fighter's mentality if you want to live a victorious and successful life in Christ. We have too many halfhearted, weak minded believers who don't know how to war in the earth and in the Spirit. There is a reason that the Israelites were unable to enter the Promised Land right after they were delivered from Egyptian bondage. There was a reason they had to go through the wilderness for 40 or so years. They lacked the mentality of a fighter.

Fighting is 90 percent mental, and the rest of it is in your head."— Anonymous

So, what does a fighter's mentality look like?

1. Hungry
2. Fearless
3. Take opportunity to go in for the kill
4. Resilient

"And from the days of John the Baptist until now the kingdom of heaven suffereth violence, and the violent take it by force." - Mathew 11:12

CHAPTER 19

Endurance with Job

Can you endure sufferings, setbacks, trials, delays, and tribulations in order to walk in greatness?

I am always intrigued and amazed when I read the story of Job and his sufferings. He truly suffered for his success. Here in America you don't hear about believers going through the same types of trials that this man went through. The Bible says,

"Now on the day when his sons and his daughters were eating and drinking wine in their oldest brother's house, a messenger came to Job and said, "The oxen were plowing and the donkeys feeding beside them, and the Sabeans attacked and took them. They also slew the servants with the edge of the sword, and I alone have escaped to tell you." While he was still speaking, another also came and said, "The fire of God fell from heaven and burned up the sheep and the servants and consumed them, and I alone have escaped to tell you." While he was still speaking, another also came and said, "The Chaldeans formed three bands and made a raid on the camels and took them and slew the servants with the edge of the sword, and I alone have escaped to tell you." While he was still speaking, another also came and said, "Your sons and your daughters were eating and drinking wine in their oldest brother's house, and behold, a great wind came from across the wilderness and struck the four corners of the house, and it fell on the young people and they died, and I alone have escaped to tell you." - Job 1:13-19

In a manner of moments Job lost his children, livestock and servants. But the onslaught wasn't finished.

"Then Satan went out from the presence of the Lord and smote Job with sore boils from the sole of his foot to the crown of his head. And he took a potsherd to scrape himself while he was sitting among the ashes. Then his wife said to him, "Do you still hold fast your integrity? Curse God and die!" But he said to her, "You speak as one of the foolish women speaks. Shall we indeed accept good from God and not accept adversity?" In all this Job did not sin with his lips." - Job 2:7-10

In another fatal swoop, Job loses his health and his wife even turned on him. I'm surprised he hadn't lost his mind and given up on God and life. Some believers today leave the church and forsake the call of God on their lives if their lights get turned off. But this man endured great suffering. Which brings up my next point that it takes endurance to run this race and walk in the abundant life that Jesus has called you to.

Endurance is defined as the fact or power of enduring an unpleasant or difficult process or situation without giving way.

Things and situations are not always going to go your way. The pieces of the puzzle will not always fit how you want them to. Doors will slam shit on you. People will leave your life and tell you no sometimes. Loved ones might forsake you and talk about you. But will you continue to press on and not give up? Or will you throw in the towel?

Imagine how Job must have felt being "that man was greatest out of all the men of the east." He was rich, successful, prestigious, honest, integral, a faithful husband and family man. But he had a huge setback, unlike any one has experienced. What he endured you only see in movies this day and time. He never gave up on God or his calling in life.

Many people have a burning desire within to achieve something great. That desire was placed in us from birth.

"The way to get started is to quit talking and begin doing."
- Walt Disney

CHAPTER 20

Stay Connected to the Vine

> "I am the true vine, and My Father is the vinedresser. Every branch in Me that does not bear fruit He [a] takes away; and every branch that bears fruit He prunes, that it may bear more fruit. You are already clean because of the word which I have spoken to you. Abide in Me, and I in you. As the branch cannot bear fruit of itself, unless it abides in the vine, neither can you, unless you abide in Me. "I am the vine, you are the branches. He who abides in Me, and I in him, bears much fruit; for without Me you can do nothing. If anyone does not abide in Me, he is cast out as a branch and is withered; and they gather them and throw them into the fire, and they are burned. If you abide in Me, and My words abide in you, you will ask what you desire, and it shall be done for you. By this My Father is glorified, that you bear much fruit; so you will be My disciples." - John 14:1-8

And they overcame him by the blood of the Lamb and by the word of their testimony, and they did not love their lives to the death. -Revelation 12:11

Many don't know they already have the victory to walk this life out in great success. The Blood of the Lamb that was shed for us gives us the overcoming power to walk in a high level of success. Our testimony of how Jesus brought us through and brought us out is the catalyst to get us from triumph to triumph. Every time you overcome some sort of obstacle in life it becomes vital that we testify about the goodness of God and how He brought about a great victory in our lives. The children of Israel would agree wholeheartedly. Look at their attitude after God brought them out of bondage and through the Red Sea.

Exodus 15:15 - "The Song of Moses"

15 Then Moses and the children of Israel sang this song to the Lord, and spoke, saying:

> "I will sing to the Lord,
> For He has triumphed gloriously!
> The horse and its rider
> He has thrown into the sea!
> The Lord is my strength and song,
> And He has become my salvation;
> He is my God, and I will praise Him;
> My father's God, and I will exalt Him.
> The Lord is a man of war;
> The Lord is His name.

Pharaoh's chariots and his army He has cast into the sea;
His chosen captains also are drowned in the Red Sea.
The depths have covered them;
They sank to the bottom like a stone.
"Your right hand, O Lord, has become glorious in power;
Your right hand, O Lord, has dashed the enemy in pieces.
And in the greatness of Your excellence
You have overthrown those who rose against You;
You sent forth Your wrath;
It consumed them like stubble.
And with the blast of Your nostrils
The waters were gathered together;
The floods stood upright like a heap;
The depths [a]congealed in the heart of the sea.
The enemy said, 'I will pursue,
I will overtake,
I will divide the spoil;
My desire shall be satisfied on them.
I will draw my sword,
My hand shall destroy them.'
You blew with Your wind,
The sea covered them;
They sank like lead in the mighty waters.
"Who is like You, O Lord, among the [b]gods?
Who is like You, glorious in holiness,
Fearful in praises, doing wonders?
You stretched out Your right hand;
The earth swallowed them.
You in Your mercy have led forth

The people whom You have redeemed;
You have guided them in Your strength
To Your holy habitation.
"The people will hear and be afraid;
Sorrow[c] will take hold of the inhabitants of Philistia.
Then the chiefs of Edom will be dismayed;
The mighty men of Moab,
Trembling will take hold of them;
All the inhabitants of Canaan will melt away.
Fear and dread will fall on them;
By the greatness of Your arm
They will be as still as a stone,
Till Your people pass over, O Lord,
Till the people pass over
Whom You have purchased.
You will bring them in and plant them
In the mountain of Your inheritance,
In the place, O Lord, which You have made
For Your own dwelling,
The sanctuary, O Lord, which Your hands have established.
"The Lord shall reign forever and ever."

For the horses of Pharaoh went with his chariots and his horsemen into the sea, and the Lord brought back the waters of the sea upon them. But the children of Israel went on dry land in the midst of the sea.

CHAPTER 21

Two Roads Diverge

> "As iron sharpens iron, so a man sharpens the countenance of his friend." - Proverbs 7:17

You will without a doubt need proper networks and the right accountability partner with you on this journey to live the abundant life. No wonder Jesus sent His disciples out in twos.

Two are better than one, because they have a good reward for their labor. For if they fall, one will lift his companion. But woe to him who is alone when he falls, for he has no one to help him up. Again, if two lie down together, they will keep warm; but how can one be warm alone? ...Ecclesiastes 4:9-12

A good accountability partner will challenge you, encourage you, warn you, and lift you up when you don't feel like taking the journey anymore.

A wise man said, "You can tell the type of person someone is by the company they keep." One of my mentor's favorite sayings is that your friends are a prophecy of your future. It really is true that "birds of a feather flock together." Maybe not at first glance, but eventually you will influence your associates, or they will influence you.

Notice that gang members and cults exercise a major influence over each other and their followers. The same trail and path one go down will be the same that others will follow. Maybe that's why Jesus asked, "If the blind lead the blind, won't they both fall into a ditch?" So, in the same way negative follows negative and the complacent follow the complacent, the successful follow the successful.

Now you might say, "I don't know any successful or famous people." That's ok because you can follow them through their books and resources. By doing this you can tap into their mind, spirit, habits, and belief systems. If you put those factors into play, you can surely have their same results. But you must start somewhere. There was a time in my own life where I had friendships with negative people who were broke, given to gossip, and jealous of those who were successful. I must admit that the same traits rubbed off on me. But I am glad I had the courage to step pin of the box, leave those old associations and seek greater in life. It has made all the difference. While studying poetry in college one poem that has stood out to me was by Robert Frost and it goes like this:

> "Two roads diverged in a yellow wood,
> And sorry I could not travel both
> And be one traveler, long I stood
> And looked down one as far as I could
> To where it bent in the undergrowth;
> Then took the other, as just as fair,

And having perhaps the better claim,
Because it was grassy and wanted wear;
Though as for that the passing there
Had worn them really about the same,
And both that morning equally lay
In leaves no step had trodden black.
Oh, I kept the first for another day!
Yet knowing how way leads on to way,
I doubted if I should ever come back.
I shall be telling this with a sigh
Somewhere ages and ages hence:
Two roads diverged in a wood, and I—
I took the one less traveled by,
And that has made all the difference."
- The Road Not Taken

The road and choices that you choose not to take will affect you for the rest of your lives. I often think about a story told by Tyron "Alimoe" Evans, an old high school basketball teammate of Rafer Alston, who was a former NBA basketball player for the Houston Rockets. He said in an interview that he had a chance to go to the same college and play collegiate basketball with Rafer but chose not to because he didn't want to discipline himself, eat right, and go to practice faithfully.

    He said after that 1st semester he regretted it because he saw the same team, he would have been on playing in the March Madness tournament on television. The same coach who wanted him to come and play there never gave him a second chance because that door had already closed. It just goes to show you that we all have the chance to upgrade our relationships and situations but if we fail to, the consequences can be devastating.

I have come to observe that there are 3 major reasons people don't upgrade their relationships to ensure their future success:

1. Fear

We fear change and the sacrifice that comes with giving up old dead and moldy acquaintances. We fear that we might be lonely, judged, and misunderstood for a season. The old saying is definitely true that "misery loves company". Some women stay in dead relationships for years with a man who devalues her goals and abilities. It takes a strong-willed person to break old acquaintances and seek for better in life.

2. Comfort

I believe comfort and complacency can cause us to stay in relationships that have clearly run their course. After a while it is time to meet new people that can shift you into a new season of discovery and aspirations.

3. Naïveté

This is the state of being naive or unable to use sound wisdom or judgment. Sometimes we are blind to the fact that our relationships are hindering our progress in life. We believe it is some unforeseen curse or internal struggle that is holding us back. When in reality our friendships are the pink elephant in the room.

CONCLUSION

Your Level of Success determines your Destiny

Just look at the lives of many great men and women who achieved their view of success. LeBron James has been hated by many and loved by many all the same. But you cannot deny that he has succeeded in his profession as an NBA basketball player. Just look at his championships, MVPs, all-star games, and fame.

Success is your portion and I pray that this book has been a blessing to you. Stay empowered in life and your success is yours for the taking in any endeavor you pursue.

> *"We've got to condition ourselves for success, for love, for breaking through our fears. And through that conditioning, we can develop patterns that automatically lead us to consistent, lifelong success."*
> *- Tony Robbins*

www.ingramcontent.com/pod-product-compliance
Lightning Source LLC
Chambersburg PA
CBHW022106170526
45157CB00004B/1500